Negotiating: Proven Strategies and Techniques

Image: Creative Commons

To Influencing People in Any Negotiation

Table of Contents

Volume 3: The Art of Negotiation – in any circumstances

Introduction

This idea of this book is to explain the whole negotiation process. Although you may not have been aware of it at the time, you may have started negotiating when you were a child. When a child comes to an agreement about the amount of pocket money he/she will receive, the child no doubt also knows that the pocket money comes as a result of something that they are expected to do. The agreement between the child and parents is usually a two way deal. Thus, negotiation takes into account the parents' expectations as well as the child's expectations. That's what negotiation is all about.

Throughout life, you are faced with situations where decisions have to be made. These don't all involve money, but they may involve more negotiation than you had really given any thought to. For example, if you agree that your wife can use the car on certain days, you are negotiating with her and coming to a conclusion that suits both of you.

Thus, when you negotiate in life, there are two sides to the story. You usually get what you want if you can give the other party something acceptable in exchange. Those who make demands without thinking about the way that the other party sees a situation are likely to fail in negotiation skills because they haven't taken account of both parties.

Communication comes into negotiation. For example, you don't get a house at a bargain price which is less than the asking price without the seller being consulted to see if the price you are offering is acceptable. He has to make a decision based on his circumstances and you on yours. This book goes through the process of communicating your intent, based on sensible negotiation criteria. Thus, you are more likely to succeed in your negotiation once these criteria have been understood and digested.

Negotiation is an art – for a few it comes natural but for others you have to learn and understand it. Whichever category you fall in, this book will enable you to successfully negotiate in circumstances you will come across and situations that happen all of a sudden. If you randomly ask a few about what negotiation is all about, the quickest answers will be related to sale and buying of a product, political negotiations and may be contract negotiations.

The book covers all kinds of situations and will help you to strengthen your negotiation skills and influence people you need to influence in order to gain something from your negotiations. Just as the child cannot expect pocket money without some form of negotiated agreement, you will get much further in your powers once you understand the basic rules and abide to them. That's where this book comes in – to help and guide you through all you need to know about negotiation.

VOLUME 1

The Art of Negotiation – the personal side of you

CHAPTER 1

Negotiating a Simple Shop Price

If you want to see how effective your negotiation skills are, then there is no better opportunity than in a shop setting. Although you can't expect to barter on prices in a supermarket, where things are tagged with the exact price, stores which sell larger items such as electrical equipment, computer equipment or furniture may just be open to some negotiation. The way that you assess this is to see if it's a small store that depend upon profits from only one outlet, or whether it's a chain store that can take the occasional loss to make a sale.

In chain stores, sometimes when a new model is brought out, the store may be left with older stock and although there may already be a sales price on the item, you could ask to speak to the manager of the particular department to see if any further reduction could be considered. It's not bad form and if the manager is trying to meet sales targets and thinks that a sale at a reduced price is better than nothing, you could get away with it.

Other circumstances where this may work is when purchasing a vehicle. In the case of a vehicle, you need to remember that on newer vehicles, you can get a reduction for doing away with some of the trim items that others may insist on. They may also be coming to the end of a promotional period and may be prepared to sell the demonstration vehicle at a reduced price. It's always worth asking.

To do this, you simply ask the Manager of the car sales company if the price marked is the very lowest that the car can be bought for. They will have already included their mark-up within that price and will know better than you what margin they have for negotiation. This works well on second hand cars. Often garages that sell new models take these in part exchange for new cars. They know exactly how much of a discount they can give and will obviously mark the vehicle with the highest price they think they can get. You can make a difference by simply asking.

In stores where you buy several items at once, it's always worthwhile asking if you can have a discount on the bundle of items that you are buying. If, for example, you are buying a dining suite and you think that you like another item, you could ask for a reduction for all of the pieces that you are interested in. Big chain stores who sell furniture are usually more interested in a bulk sale and will often be open to negotiating a price with you.

So how do you negotiate?

A straight approach is the best approach and it gives you an honest answer quickly. Simply find the member of staff who manages the department where you want to make an offer. When you have located that person, simply ask in the manner shown below, showing no hesitation at all. It's good to be friendly in your approach.

"I was wondering. If I bought this item and that item together, does your company give a discount?"

It's straightforward and their answer will be straightforward too. If they say "No" you can simply go elsewhere if you still think that the price is too high. One thing that they may offer you which may be worthwhile considering is interest free credit. This is often worth thinking about because instead of paying huge amounts of interest on the amount you spend for the items in question, you can spread the payments over a set amount of time and still pay the same as you would have paid had you paid in one lump sum. Although this isn't a reduction as such, it does give you more money in your pocket at the time of purchase and make paying for the item much easier. If they do have interest free credit, they will no doubt tell you, rather than lose your custom altogether.

Negotiation means knowing your options. If in doubt, or wanting to save money, there are other tips which can help you to do this. You may have heard of Price Promise schemes. Often shops pit themselves against the competition by offering deals on items that they believe you cannot match elsewhere. If you think that the price looks expensive, there is nothing to stop you from looking elsewhere and doing price comparisons. If you can come up with details of another shop that offer the same item at a lower price, you can save yourself money and take advantage of their price promise. You do need to have specific details so that they can check, but if you are sure of your facts, you may be able to negotiate the price of the item down based on the fact that it is offered elsewhere at a lower price.

CHAPTER 2

Negotiating the Price of a House

This is probably going to be one of the largest purchases that you make in your life. Thus, how much you can negotiate the sales price will matter to you. You need to keep various things in mind when negotiating on a house price. One of these is how long the house has been for sale. A desperate seller who has had their house on the market for a long time will be more likely to accept a lower price. They will have moved on in their lives and perhaps want to close off a chapter of their lives. The house may be stopping them from doing this.

Looking at the house in question, you need to put yourself in a powerful negotiation situation by looking at things which may give you leverage over the price you pay. For example, the following items need to be borne in mind:

- How much can you borrow?

- How much is the house worth compared with other houses which are similar?

- How much will it cost you to do any repairs?

- How soon can you purchase?

- How long has the house been on the market?

We have already mentioned the last item, though you will need to set up your finances so what you know what you can afford. This puts you in a much stronger position to negotiate for a very good reason. Supposing that two potential sellers made a bid on a house but one had the finances and one was speculative and was with a potential purchaser that hadn›t sorted out what they could actually borrow. Any sensible homeowner who is selling a house would choose the purchaser with financing in place. They want a sure thing rather than a speculative one.

If you work it out, over the course of the house having been for sale, they will have no doubt seen many potential purchasers who turned out to be time-wasters. From the point of view of the seller, until you actually have solid financing, you could potentially be wasting their time. It›s unlikely, in these circumstances that they would want to negotiate with you, since what you offer is speculative at best. This is a big event for them as well, so make sure you are in a stronger position by having already talked to your bank and by knowing what the bank will lend you and what you can afford.

Comparisons

To strengthen your side of the bargaining, you need to know that what they are offering is a fair price. Shopping the market helps you to do this. Look for houses with similar features and see if they are in the same price range, within the same geographical area. This helps you to bring more to the negotiation table. For example, if you know that the price is high for the area, then chances are that they do too. A comparison helps you to give a strong offer and to let them know that you cannot offer more since there are other houses within your price range which offer more for less.

The repair question

This comes into the equation as well. If a house needs fixing up, you need to know that you can afford the house and the repairs that are needed to bring it up to a standard which you find acceptable. The seller needs to know what you think and will already be aware that perhaps they haven't been as careful as owners as they should have been. They offer you a house at a price and you have to decide what the cost of repairs would be and what value this would add to the house. If they are selling the house cheap because it needs repairs, then there isn't much room for negotiation. If they are not, then you can show them the prices you come up with for the relevant repairs and ask for a reduction in the price to allow you to effect these repairs.

A reasonable person will accept that the house only has a set value. If you have to pay the top price and then add to the expense by doing repairs, you need to add up the total and see if the house, in good repair, will bring in the equivalent of what you have spent. If it will not, then use this as justification for a reduction in price.

They may ask you how quickly you can move. This may matter to them since they may be making mortgage payments and want to know that you can move pretty rapidly so that they save money on those payments. If you can be in a position where you are ready to move that quickly, they may also be happy to give you a reduction to be sure that the sale actually goes through. The house may be a noose around their necks that they need to get rid of and if you are not in a position to move fast, they may sell it to someone who is.

CHAPTER 3

The Two Sides of a Negotiation Table

As you have learned from previous chapters, negotiations don›t just depend upon your skill to make an offer. They depend upon two people coming to an agreement. Whether that›s for a car, a household item or for the house itself, both sides need to be considered. You give yourself more power in the negotiations if you can remember this. The shop that sells you a cheaper TV may do so if they need to make the sale to meet sales figures. If they don›t then try another store and find one that does. That bargaining power depends upon it. In the case of car, a car showroom may sell you a second hand car that they have taken in exchange for a new one, but they are not going to take less than they paid for it, or lost when they sold the new car. They will have given the purchaser a reduction against the car that you are about to buy. They know their margins and you need to ask the right questions in order to get a deal. Be outright and be honest, and if the deal isn›t to your liking, walk away.

For every situation in life where negotiation is required, you need to work out what›s in it for both parties. If you want that car at a reduced price, what›s in it for the garage? What about the house you want to buy? Did you think about why the owner may sell it cheaper? You need to estimate the risk of making an offer and be ready with a counter-offer if your initial offer is not acceptable. In this situation, you also need to be sure on how much you are willing to spend and to stop all negotiations when that amount is reached. You may just be surprised when the seller of a house comes back to you and says you can have the house, even though he initially refused your offer. It›s a game between two parties. He may have thought that you were not putting all of your cards on the table. The silence after the rejection will make him rethink if he can afford to sell it for the price you offered. He may even come back with a counter offer that you can somehow reach.

Negotiation for anything requires establishing the goal that you are aiming for, working out what›s in it for the other party and working out how much you can afford to offer in exchange for their agreement. The same works when you are negotiating for anything, regardless of whether this includes a monetary reward.

Take a look at this situation. A secretary wants a pay rise. She isn›t doing any more than she has been doing for the past two years. Thus, she doesn›t really merit one on the basis of the work she does. If she asks for a pay rise, she is going to get refused because there is nothing in it for the employer except perhaps having a happier employee. If she were to approach the situation differently she may actually swing the decision in her favor. Examining the needs of the office, she could decide that there is something more that she can do that would be a real service to the office in general. For example, she may have observed problem areas where her help would make things run in a smoother way. If she used this when she went to the negotiation table, the boss would then see that perhaps there is something in it for the company. It won›t always work, but it›s a better bet than simply going to the negotiation table demanding something and offering nothing extra in exchange.

Even from childhood, negotiations need to be two sided. A child wants to go to an overnight party. He uses the excuse that he is staying at a friend›s house. The parents want something in exchange before they agree. They want the telephone number of the parents of the child he says he is staying with. The child may kick up a fuss and refuse to give this, although the parents would then be within their rights to refuse the child. That›s the way negotiation works and the negotiation table has two sides to it.

The same scenario happens in an electrical shop, where the TV you want is the last one that they have on display. They don›t have any boxed units left and you either have to wait for one to be delivered or you could ask in a friendly way if you could have the TV on display at a lower price because it›s actually been "used." It's also a good time to joke about the dust that's on it coming free in the package, because sales people do have a sense of humor and you can always use this to win favor without insulting the goods that they are selling. If you do see slight damage on an item, you can show them this in a friendly way and ask if there is a reduction because of the damage. It may even be something so small that you can wipe it off when you get home! The shop will want to get rid of defective items and so there is something on the bartering table for them as well as for you!

CHAPTER 4

Negotiating in a Relationship

The influence that you have on another person largely depends upon your approach. Mutual respect always works better than demands. A husband that demands that his wife stays at home and does not work is exercising a lack of understanding if indeed his wife wants to work. Thus, there are not two sides to the negotiation table and he is forcing her to do something that she is not happy doing.

With any situation in a human relationship, whether it›s with your boss, employees, and friendships or with people within your family, there has to be this two sided respect. If you want to achieve something, you have to work out in your mind how you can put the idea forward taking into account the other person›s feelings on the matter and offer something that is satisfactory to both parties. Without this respect you will never be a good negotiator. It is actually easier to learn than you may imagine.

Ask a child to do something that they don›t like doing and you will get some form of resentment or even negativity. The child will not want to do something that is not in their interest. However, make that task tempting and they will do it gladly. That›s not suggesting you use bribes, but that you use the "carrot and stick" trick that means that at the end of doing that task, something else follows that they actually really want. By doing that, you achieve what you want but you also put something worthwhile onto the negotiation table.

You want Friday night out with the lads. She is a little reticent about the idea because she is possessive and doesn't want you to be out chasing girls. The negotiation skill works here. She may equally be looking to do something by herself. This may be having gym classes with friends or inviting friends over that you don't particularly like. How about suggesting she use the evenings you go out to have those friends round and have a really good girly evening? It doesn't have to be exactly that, but you do need to put something on the negotiation table so that they will accept your wishes and see them as beneficial to everyone, not just you.

Adults have to make decisions all of the time for children because the children are too young to make those decisions for themselves. In the adult world, without the supervision of parents, people who are looking for independence can't just demand it. They need to prove that they are capable of that independence. For example, if a child wants to leave home, all a parent wants to know is that the child is safe. Thus, the child needs to put up the argument that they have thought out how they will be able to survive, to pay their bills and to live as an adult. That's basically all that the child needs to put on the negotiation table to get agreement. In a similar way, when you want to do something as an adult and something is holding you back, look at the situation, examine it from other perspectives and work out a way that you can achieve it without resistance by using negotiation powers that give everyone a satisfactory result.

Negotiation with clients

This is a different situation, but in a way, the same structure occurs. You offer something to a client and they need to decide whether what you offer is worth their while investing in. To make a sale work, you need to apply the same rules as above. Be amiable, get to know the client and get to know their needs. Once you do, you will be able to fit what you are offering into their needs bracket and thus give them something of value, as weighed up against other companies with sales staff who offer very little. The personal attention to detail is everything when it comes to negotiation and you are much more likely to succeed if you remember the equation:

Your needs on one side of the table – Their needs on the other = Positive result.

Now look at it from another perspective. You offer something that a client wants, but he already knows he can get it cheaper elsewhere. How could you make your offer more attractive? The thing is that you can if you can think of some way of making the negotiations more attractive. Perhaps you can give loyalty discounts. Perhaps you can deliver more quickly than the other company. Perhaps your goods come with a better guarantee or better after sales service. People are prepared to pay more for those aspects and by using your negotiation rules as shown above, you fit their needs better than by simply offering a more expensive service or product without using the negotiation skill of defining the difference between the cheaper product and yours.

CHAPTER 5

Influencing People

Your attention to detail will influence people, whether in the workplace or in personal relationships. The fact that you have thought things through really does help people to have more confidence in you and gives you a chance to influence them. In business, your influence may come from the respect that you give people you meet. This mutual respect is also a part of the negotiation question because if you appear to be disrespectful, dress inappropriately or behave in a way which is an embarrassment to your company, you give the other people that you meet the impression that you have less to offer them. Thus, mutual respect includes dressing appropriately, treating people in the right way and behaving in a manner which is likely to gain respect and also to influence any decisions which are to be made.

Imagine a salesman who turns up late, forgets his sales pitch and treats the customer like the appointment is an inconvenience in their day. They are hardly likely to be impressed with that approach. Now, imagine the salesman who telephones to confirm that the appointment is still on, who gets to know his client and his client›s needs, who takes a personal interest in his client and goes out of his way to be polite and accommodating. He is much more likely to gain influence when it comes to the company making decisions. Thus, what the successful salesman has taken to the negotiation table is not only a product, but friendly approach, professional courtesy and politeness. That makes him much more powerful.

It›s not just in business either. If you want to buy something at a knock down price in a market or a garage sale, have some respect for the seller. Of course, a seller wants to make money, but if you insult the seller by offering too low a price, you may just stop him from selling you the item. Many people make this mistake. Think what the item is worth, think of what would be a bargain price and then think of why the seller is selling the item and how much they will lose in the deal. Most garage sales items are already at rock bottom prices and you can still strike a wonderful deal without alienating the seller. Being reasonable always works better than being rude.

This book is about winning in negotiations and using tactics to do so, but it›s also about your influence over others. Honest negotiations help people to have confidence in you. For example, if you know that all you can offer for that car is $5,500 then you need to tell the salesman that it›s your best offer. You can start lower, because you don›t know what his situation is. For example, he may have had that car on the lot for ages and be glad to see the back of it. It may be taking up valuable space on his prime lot and he may be perfectly willing to part with it for less than the price tag. However, once you reach your limit, you need to say to him.

"I'm afraid that's all that I have." and walk away if he wants more. You will gain more respect by being honest and not wasting his time. He may just turn around and accept your offer because you didn't waste his time and he needs the sale. If you mess him around playing the part of the know-it-all, he may just be irked enough to let you have no influence over his decision. Negotiation isn't just about you and your ego. It's about the mutual feelings of two parties about to shake hands on a deal which suits them both.

Similarly, when you offer a homeowner a price on their house, you can influence their decision by backing up your offer and showing them that you are serious and have a bank loan already arranged. The influence that this has is that they know you are a serious buyer and not someone who was just curious enough to want to look around their home.

Body language in negotiations

Although you may not be aware of it, your body may be giving different messages to other people. It's wise to brush up on your skills at presenting yourself. For example, if you cannot look someone in the eye over the negotiation table, they are unlikely to trust you. If you want to influence their decision try to get out of the habit of looking down or away from people when you are talking to them. It won't help your bargaining power.

Other body language which is unhelpful is nervousness. This puts people on edge and makes them think that you have ulterior motives rather than merely wanting to negotiate something important to you. Crossing your arms gives out the impression that you are not open to listening and in the process of negotiations can be very unhelpful.

Remember that negotiation is used even with your children. It's a skill that you learn as you go through life. If you demand that your children do certain things, you are much more likely to get a response if they know there's something enjoyable in it for them. A child told to read out loud from the newspaper could actually read the times of his favorite show, thus use reading as an exercise to gain access to knowledge which helps him. A boss who you want to approach for a pay rise also needs some justification to give that pay rise. In all walks of life, negotiation takes two people and as long as that is always borne in mind when you go to the negotiation table, you won't go far wrong. So what do you do if your skills don't work? You learn from it what you did wrong and walk away. You keep your head up high and learn that perhaps your approach needs changing the next time. It's about growth of personality but once your powers of persuasion increase, you will find you will be doing this less and less and that you are able to persuade people that the deal is worthwhile.

VOLUME 2

---

*The Art of Negotiation – the business
side of you*

CHAPTER 6

Realizing the Power of Negotiation

Negotiations play a vital role in our personal and professional lives. In our personal lives, we negotiate our ways with our friends, family and neighbors. And particularly if it involves any decision making which may have unexpected outcomes then it will surely require negotiation skills at various levels. Some situations that we come across frequently:

- Neighbors – if you have a piece of land that has a common space in between
- You feel going to a party is important while most of others in the family don't think so
- You have plans of setting up an event and your friend has different ways of doing it
- Kids – discipline, completing homework and allowing them to play

Irrespective of the situation whether it's supporting the situation or resisting it – the fact is you are negotiating.

The different forms of Negotiation

To negotiate and differentiate better, you need to understand the different types or forms of negotiations that usually you will come across. In each of these types, you will have to take different approaches and strategy in order to successfully negotiate. By understanding the forms of negotiations you will be able to visualize the next possible situation that may arise.

Combined Negotiations

You might come across situations where you know both sides of the coin, rather whom you are negotiating. And if you compromise in certain aspects you would know that there will be a win-win for both the parties involved. Combined negotiations are situations where either parties are open to what each has to say and settle down in between where both of them are happy.

It is purely based on how well you are willing to understand and listen to what each one has to say. In this type of negotiations, you will get what you want without sacrificing or compromising too much. There will resolution to any type of problem as both parties involved will be able to form a common consent. In this type of negotiation issues are prioritized and dealt. The topmost issues are resolved with mutual consent to arrive at a logical conclusion and the other issues are either ignored or left out as they may not create any impact.

Even before the negotiation starts, information from either parties involved is shared so that everyone understands the reason behind the negotiation. Most of the problems get resolved as information is shared with positive intentions. In Combined negotiations success depends on trust factor. Both parties and everyone involved, trust each other's decision and will tend to abide by what is said and done.

Fixed Negotiations

In this type of negotiations everyone would like to have their share. Fixed negotiations essentially do not mean that there is limited or fixed scope, instead the parties involved will have a fixed mindset while dealing in such situations. Either parties involved will not be keen to share information and will try to get information as much as possible from the other party.

They will first want to make the other person make the offer and check how it will affect them. The negotiations in this type happen only after gathering information. Once the individual who gathers enough information is satisfied then they will negotiate from a position of strength. Emotions are not let out so easily, so the other person in the situation will not know what you are going through. This type of negotiation will work well when you wish to buy a product and are trying to get maximum information from the sales person before you make the decision of buying it.

And once the information is obtained, you will wait till the other party makes an offer. It so happens that once the target is met then the offer made will be so near to what you expected in your mind.

The different stages of Negotiation

The different stages of negotiation explain the process involved in negotiation and how to deal in each stage. Each stage of negotiation is further elaborated in the coming chapters. These different stages of negotiation, clearly explain the parties involved, types of information that is exchanged and closing the deal once it is negotiated. All the phases in negotiation are important and are interlinked with each other.

Information Interchange

Exchanging information between all the parties is the first step in any kind of information. If either parties involved or even one party doesn't know what they are getting into, the process of negotiation fizzles out even before it takes off. As a first step information exchange plays a crucial role in setting up the much needed platform the parties involved to understand and set expectations from the negotiation and the outcome.

The information exchanged could be in any form of communication or it may even happen if one party is involved. For example, if you are planning to buy a mobile phone – instead of asking too many questions to the sales guy, you may even keep silence by forcing him to say everything and make him interested in selling the phone to you.

And if your kid wants to play without completing homework, you can then explain or give information about how both things can happen. So that they have information on hand about what might happen next.

Bargaining

There are many ways you could bargain in a given situation. The next important step before you actually think of buying something is bargaining. Now that the information is exchanged, understood and considered you may explore to the next level of expressing what you would need.

To bargain effectively, it is very much important that you have all the necessary tools and information. Bargaining can happen by letting the other party know what your intention is, or just wait for the right moment till the other party makes the first move. Either ways, your objective is to get your point through.

Closing

After the first two steps are completed, this is where most of the deals either get delayed or never happen. Like negotiation is an art, closing is the master piece of it. You may have the best information in the world and appreciation for the product and you also do a good job in finalizing the price you want it – what if you don't own it or get it later.

It's like the salesman who has projected a sale in his quarter based on the assumptions and finally the sale did not happen because you didn't buy it or the contract wasn't signed in the stipulated time. And till such time it doesn't happen, it stands that the deal is not closed.

Expertise in Negotiation

In the first place, negotiation happens because none of them involved would want to arrive at a consensus. To negotiate well you would need to have a balanced approach and understand various factors that are involved in negotiations. In the chapters coming by, negotiation skills for success are further discussed. The following skills/statements will keep you in position of strength and enable you to succeed in any kind of negotiation.

- Listen to what others have to say, before you jump into the conversation
- Being creative
- A good sense of humor
- Being patient and assess the whole situation
- Never give up attitude
- Giving space and appreciate what others have to say
- Determination and confidence that you can get through

To develop these skills you need to understand what each statement means and how it should be dealt. If you are the first one to speak and would not want the other person to speak then you will never get into a consensus as the other person will never open up. If you feel that the information exchange is quite dull and needs a bit of fresh air, you should find out creative ways to approach the situation, give some out of the box ideas to make it happen.

You may even share a joke related to the situation and make sure that the other side doesn't mind as long as it is in control. The deal may happen today or tomorrow, but the most important trait you need to carry is patience and an attitude of not giving up. By doing so, you will win it for sure. Make the other party involved also feel that you are serious about the entire thing. With enough confidence on your side, your aim should only be focused towards closing the deal and considering all the above statements mentioned.

CHAPTER 7

Preparing yourself – Negotiating circumstances

Before you enter into any situation it requires a lot of preparation. And if it is negotiation then you need to understand the possible outcomes, what is acceptable for you and what is not acceptable. You need to understand all the challenges that you may face and plan to tackle them accordingly. Apart from preparing for the negotiation based on certain criteria, you have to prepare yourself. When you enter into a negotiation, it is important that you proceed forward with lots of confidence and a winning attitude.

If you do not have the right attitude, you may not appreciate the entire situation and will not be able to justify the end to end result. You may also end up in getting a result that may not be the desired one. You need to work out the right balance between what is acceptable to the parties and getting the best result.

The worst and best situations

Most of the times, in negotiations either parties are carried away by assuming that the end result will be the way they have envisaged. And they are absolutely not sure about the alternatives of a particular outcome if it doesn't happen. So since they have already assumed certain outcome they are not willing to look at other options what the negotiation has to offer. They finally become so fixed in their ideas that they do not see any option out. And if you do not know the best possible options and the worst possible options that may happen in an agreement after negotiation you will never know how it all ends.

It is necessary that both parties involved in the negotiation have to decide about how the desired outcome is going to be. The worst and best situations in a negotiated agreement have to be thought much earlier. This will allow either parties to look at all possibilities of a win-win situation.

In case if you feel that the possibility of a situation doesn't arise at all in negotiation, you may feel why to focus on such a situation in the first place. However it is important to understand that reality may be something else than what we assume. If everything is so well crafted in the Universe, then probably we may not have earthquakes, disasters and people dying for no reason. You should always think close to reality and make sure that you know that every situation has a worst scenario while thinking positive about it.

You should have your answers ready for the 'what if' situations if something goes the opposite way from what you had originally planned. By realizing the fact that something worst may happen you will be able to understand how adaptable you could be in a situation that could pop up all of a sudden. At any given point of time getting into a best situation is always beneficial when compared to getting into a worst situation. But it all depends on how well you envisage these situations when you actually start negotiating.

Negotiations happen to make sure a consensus is arrived and the deal is closed ultimately. So being either in the worst situation or the best situation, since you had already prepared yourself for these kind of scenarios your job will be to negotiate well and get a result of your choice.

The final verdict

In the process of negotiation it is extremely important that you have a price in mind that you would finalize on. You may negotiate the price of something for various reasons, but the most obvious reason would be to reduce the price of the initial offer made. On the contrary, you need to be cautious to hide your feelings if you would like to take the product at any cost. If you do that you will not be negotiating from a position of strength, especially when the other party notices it.

You need to have a set price in mind and have a positive approach when you make the final verdict on the price part. The other side, they may try to get into an unfavorable discussion to make sure you take a decision in their favor. But if you are strong on your final verdict and be firm on the price, you will walk away with what you intend to.

Imagine if it is a property for which the other party wants to pay you less, you may settle down for less considering what other value adds you get for the compromise you made regarding the price. And at the same time, the other party will also look at what is the best price they can offer. Their whole idea would be to sell the product or service and to do so, they will look at possible ways where they can cut down on the price and where they can't. Ultimately they would want the product or the service to be sold.

It is like pulling the rubber band string too much. It is extremely important that you will not negotiate so hard that the deal is put off. Either parties will make sure they keep everything to themselves before letting it go. And this should happen till the time you want to negotiate in certain set limits and then let go, only to make sure the deal is struck.

The other important aspect in negotiation is that you will let the other party know that you can walk out of the deal at any given point of time. This feeling will become strong when you have a set price in your mind, before the actual negotiation starts. In spite of your other party getting this feeling about your thoughts, they will still try to do all sorts of things so that they get at least something or the other before they let go. And you are put to test to see how much you could resist in the negotiation process.

While you decide on the final verdict and a fix price in your mind, it is essential that you don't set any unrealistic price to it. By doing so, the other party will have numerous questions at each stage of the negotiation and the deal is dragged forever.

What you are willing to consider

Before the negotiation starts both parties should hope that there is a consensus where everyone involved is satisfied. When a house is sold, both the parties should be happy based on the final outcome. Most of the times, whatever price is estimated may not be possible but if you have a minimum price that you wouldn't want to go down then it is still a reason to be satisfied.

In real life situation, you will have to understand that whatever you expect in an ideal situation or a fantasy situation will not happen. The price that is fixed for the product or the service should be as per the norms of the market and at an acceptable limit. From this perspective you may do some minor adjustments to your fixed price in mind. The other extreme you should also make sure that beyond a limit there is no point in negotiating further. At this juncture, you may even walk away from the deal itself. Fix both these points before the start and end of the negotiation.

The same thinking will apply to the opposite party with whom you deal with. Both the parties start off with an indicative price range where the negotiation starts. Most of the times it so happens that the price which your party wants to offer will be far off to what you actually expect. In any circumstances, you should not let the other party know that you are willing to close the deal at a certain price, before the negotiation starts.

Tips to prepare yourself – while negotiating

☐ One way to relieve some of the tension you may be feeling before negotiation is to remind yourself that there is nothing to be afraid of.

As long as you understand your position, there is no danger that you will lose the negotiation. During and before negotiation you should always be:

- Well-mannered – By being so, it doesn't mean that your argument is null
- Stable – Removes perception of weakness
- Composed – Facilitates persuasion and compromise
- Do try to take anything personally

Knowing your position before entering into negotiations means that you are sure of where to start and how to end. Things that you are not prepared to consider that would make your position worse than it is now. Many people get forced themselves into a deal which is not satisfactory to them because they have not succeeded to prepare themselves for the negotiation. If you get into a negotiation without specific agenda the negotiation will position you on a weak stance.

The most important factor in negotiation is that you should be the only one who knows what it is. The moment your opposite party knows that you are positioning yourself from a desperate position then it will never go your way. And assumptions are made that you are willing to buy it for any price as you need it at any cost.

CHAPTER 8

Battlefield – Keeping your forces ready

In the previous chapters you have seen how to bargain in a situation from a position of strength. To prepare for the best outcome you need to keep all the necessary tools ready so that you do not miss out on the best opportunity. You need to create and adhere to certain principles that will help you in the negotiation process at an early stage. It may sound as if you have to go through lot of documentation, setting up framework and strengthening your thought process – whatever it may be, it is the first important step to be ready before the actual take off.

Choose the venue and the time

If you are in a position to choose the venue and time for negotiation you will have an edge over others. You will feel positive if the negotiation is conducted at your chosen place and you will make sure to complete the deal with more vigor. You could also chose a time and date for the negotiation to start that could be in your favor. On the contrary there could be lot of other factors that could hinder the negotiation if the venue is not set up properly. These factors could even spoil the entire process and even put off the deal in certain cases.

- Periodical interventions by outsiders
- Sound pollution from nearby areas
- Too many people getting involved
- No focus due to privacy issues

So if you make sure that the negotiation happens at your chosen destination, then you could have control of each and every situation that you may come across. But if you do the same thing at the venue chosen by the other party, you may not even know the consequences and the remedy if something goes awry.

If it is a negotiation that involves a political situation, due to the sensitivity the venue is usually neutral. Any one side advantage could lead to a disaster and will end up usually with no result. A neutral venue is chosen, because neither of them will have no idea of how the surroundings will shape up. Whereas in business negotiations choosing a neutral venue may not be a right option as no party will have control on the other.

A home team advantage – In sports, the team that plays on their home turf will naturally have advantage if the other team is playing there for the first time. No one would know it better than the home team regarding the turns and pitfalls when it comes to the game. By the time the other team spends time in understanding the surroundings the game is all over.

Timing – This is extremely important in negotiations. Everyone has their own timing to which they would like to adjust the entire day's proceedings. The body gets tuned to certain time periods and will work well at certain timings. You cannot do some deal at an odd time when your body is completely exhausted and you feel like just sleeping. Check when your mind is fresh to take up a challenging task like negotiation. The early compromises will start from here, when both the parties discuss about the time and venue. In such cases, you should make a strong pitch regarding the time and venue and if doesn't happen, make sure that you get something else on this behalf.

Pulling the strings together

Often both the parties that are involved in negotiation tend to discuss about issues and aspects that are not of immediate priority. So they feel that the process is heading positively and they are really working hard to conclude, where the real fact is it is not happening that way. Rather it is important to start the negotiation based on what is agreed prior and take it off from there. After discussing on a common ground, then you may look at the tougher ones that need to be resolved. You need to first test the waters of the other party involved and get acquainted with the situations and then take up the tougher ones because you have made the ground already.

By taking up this approach you move in a positive direction as it is step wise. You will also make sure that there is a common approach and a goal that is developed with this kind of approach. Setting the tone and pace is very important in negotiations. If the meetings are continuously disrupted by external forces or are dragged by never ending conversations, the pace and tone is lost.

To create a positive impact, it is essential that an agenda is set that is full of positive energy and a pace that determines what to expect next. If both the parties involved agree upon a framework then there could be lot of considerations that can happen. The only point you need to look at is if you consider something what will you lose and what will you gain. If all the loose ends are tied together then you will have an edge over the other party and can make the negotiation evolve into a favorable result.

The negotiation charter

A charter is a framework that is designed to make sure negotiations happen on a set platform. Both parties involved in negotiations will have their own set of rules and a design based on which they come prepared for the negotiations. This framework should be designed based on your objectives, values and your past experience in dealing with situations like these. Any issue that is discussed will have its affect while the negotiation is happening. If you get carried away by how these issues have shaped up then you will tend to move away from your original goal.

Most of the time is spent on talking and discussing about how to go about. Instead focus should be laid on the most important things to discuss and the least important things that should be ignored. At the same time, it is also important that what areas you are willing to consider and what areas you will not. If that is frozen then discussion on a particular topic will be more focused. You would then know what words and statements to use in the permissive limits and what points should be avoided.

If there is no agenda or a charter then every discussion that is part of the negotiation will be shot in a different direction. And memories only last for a while, but if you have everything thought through before then it will be easy to work on the set platform. You need to make sure that the framework set for negotiations is positive. Otherwise most of the times, either parties get impatient on certain points and they would like to give it enough time before the dust settles in.

Negotiation process – elaborated from previous chapters

In the previous chapters you have understood the important elements of the negotiation process and how to make sure there is a step wise approach in dealing with these elements. Now you will understand these points more elaborately for making sure the process is dealt positively under any circumstances. The stepwise process is summarized below for your understanding.

- Preparing yourself – based on what you need and your intentions.
- Getting started
  - Understand the overall situation of the negotiation.
  - Decide the price range and how to play within the range.
  - Make sure that the pricing and other factors are realistic and achievable.
  - Make sure that there is flexibility in the approach you take.
  - Finalize on the end points and agreements that need to be reached.
- Approach towards bargaining

- Where ever necessary ask for more information and make sure you get it.
- Question the other party and challenge them on points that needs justification.
- Make the other party understand about how committed you are.
- Discussions that take place during bargaining should be closed amicably
- Identify indicative factors and work accordingly.
- Prepare a common platform for the bargaining to take place.
- Moving forward
  - Allow the other party to express before you zero in on what you have to say.
  - Make sure the discussion starts with low priority issues and then move to the high priority issues.
  - Don't compromise more than what you can.
  - Any considerations made during the negotiations should be used as an advantage
  - Any discussion that takes place from your end should have certain clauses. It should not be a broad discussion ending nowhere or accepting everything what others have to say.
  - Anything you take forward should be realistic in nature and as per what you originally thought.
  - You may have to consider certain aspects in the initial stages as it allows the other party to build trust in you. So be open towards it.
  - Make small steps to take the necessary leap later.
- Deal closing
  - Make sure both the parties involved understand the benefits and proceeds of the deal.

- Before you close the deal, you should make sure that the other party understands the consequences or losses if an agreement is not reached. And it should be communicated in an indirect way or subtle way.
- Do not drag any discussion till it tears apart. Instead make sure there is a rhythm and timing to what you do.
- Take essential care while you make the final offer and make sure it is on the lines of what you originally thought of (without much deviation).
- Make sure that any agreement that is finalized between parties is understood well.
- Document whatever is necessary.
- Exchange information and documents once the deal is closed.

CHAPTER 9

Information Interchange – to and fro

An important phase of negotiation is exchanging information that is very crucial for the deal to make or break. And it is important for you to know what to reveal and when to reveal. Too much of information in the initial stages also could lead to the other party knowing everything about you. In such cases, the other party may have an advantage as they know too many things about you. At the same time, less information about you also is dangerous, as the other party may not know whom they are dealing with and why they should deal.

By allowing them to know about you, they will understand at what level you are currently at. And they will also know your position of strength. Without understanding and realizing the situation it will be difficult for you to start the negotiation process.

On your mark, get set go

Even before you start off, it is important to get acquainted with the other people involved in the negotiation and find out if there is anything common between both of you. And if you are not able to do this, you may give an impression to the other party that you are looking at closing the deal at the earliest even without exchanging favorable notes. It is still acceptable in certain circumstances but is not the best way to deal as far as negotiations are concerned.

By introducing yourself and exchanging some common notes you will only find it advantageous to you. The other party will know how much you consider this deal and what kind of space you will offer to them for making the negotiation pleasantry. And by doing it this way, you will break the ice in an informal way and set the tone for being formal when the actual negotiation takes place. Make sure that you know important details like their name, occupation, background and their ethnic details if they are international parties with different culture.

When you are on the mark and ready to go, the first stride you take is very important as it will decide whether you will win the race or not. For this to happen, you should create an impression to the other party that you are friendly and would like to make sure that the deal works out in favor of both. Even if the deal doesn't happen due to certain external factors your exit will be smooth as the other party understands that you did not do anything intentionally. And if there is a scope in the future regarding a similar deal or with the same party they would be still open to look at you as a strong option.

What to say and what not to say

Make sure that you don't make any statements before the start of negotiation. Never open regarding what you are going through and never display your weakness if you have any. Imagine, if the other party forces you into a situation that may not be important for the moment, you may subtly tell them to discuss about this later. By saying so, you will make them focus on the most important things that are necessary for the negotiation.

And also try to understand why the other person is hurrying up to get to where you are. If you know that then you may both choose to compromise and consider or you may think of an alternative strategy. If they are hurrying it may even work to your advantage as they will be keen to give it away at any cost.

The secret within you

Keep the secrets with you and don't let them unfold till the deal is closed. Keeping too much to yourself also could be an issue as the other party may feel you are hiding too much. But it all depends on how you portray yourself as a transparent person. To make sure there is transparency on all sides it is important that you set an agenda based on the points to discuss further. This way both of you know what to discuss and what to divulge.

In the initial stages both of you may be hesitating to divulge information, but someone needs to take the lead to have the edge in the negotiation. By setting an agenda and not letting too much information out, certain issues are resolved even before the process gets started. When you negotiate your success clearly depends on three aspects – when to say, what to say and staying silent when it matters most.

CHAPTER 10

Proven techniques in negotiation - Bargaining & Closing

In the previous chapters you have read briefly how bargaining, negotiating and closing is done. Now the same process is explained elaborately to help you out in dealing with actual situations. Bargaining is considered to be the heart of any negotiation process. This chapter explains about what situations you could expect when bargaining and if something goes awry how to deal with it. Negotiators use something called common bargaining methods and you will know more about this in this chapter.

In this chapter you will understand more about negotiations pertaining to techniques and agreements that you could reached. And finally, the last phase of the negotiation is closing. You have to put all your efforts to make sure that both the parties reach consensus. You will feel that it is happening when statements exchange like "so we have reached an agreement".

Knowing what you are getting into

While you enter into negotiation it is important to understand the negotiation style and techniques of your opposite party. You may want to know the following information before you proceed any further:

- Are they people who start off some unreasonable offer or do not know what they are talking about
- Are they pushing it too hard and hurrying up
- Are they portraying issues pertaining to negotiation to their advantage

It may not be easy to know all these, but you should find out a way to know all these before the actual negotiation takes place. By knowing your opposite party's strength & weakness you can analyze the situation better and turn it to your favor. And when you finally set the negotiation platform this information will be very handy.

Testing the waters

There are many techniques which you could use for making the negotiation successful. The most common ones are based on two situations:

The hope of happening: Imagine you have a set price of $500 in mind and the other party has made an offer that is way beyond your expectation which is $1500. Then you may think that since $500 is too low, you may wish to settle down for about $1000 which is a bit too high. If you are experienced in negotiations you will know that this is exaggerating and wouldn't allow something like this to happen.

A price you will pay now and later it may change: The other technique your opposite party could use is that they will make you feel that if you buy the product it is $1000 and buying it next week could cost you $2000. There may be truth or no truth at all, you will fall easy for such kind of technique as you want one and wouldn't like to spend so much on it. Or the party may even flatter you by saying that it is only because they like you they are offering this price. In any situation, if you have a firm belief and control over the situation you will not fall prey to such techniques.

Some more techniques are mentioned below:

- There is no second choice – prepare well that's it.
- Be attentive and have a good timing for negotiation and closing the deal.
- Do not be egoistic
- Understand what the other party has to say

- Ask and you shall get, don't feel shy and don't hide your feelings
- Be prepared to consider certain aspects
- Be committed and make the other party also committed
- Don't try to look too deep into their problems and take it on your shoulders

If nothing happens what next

If the negotiation is stuck at some point and doesn't move forward you need to try something like these and make sure it moves forward in the desired direction:

- If the reason it is stuck involves some money, then make sure you come up with ideas like changing the terms of negotiation and making it as a short term return or make it long term return based on how it may move forward.
- Try and change the team or its member and check how it works now.
- Make some small sacrifices to make sure it moves forward and you may later on hold on to the bigger ones.
- Check out the options you had earlier and try to change a few.
- If it not moving any further, agree upon a fixed time to get back to the issue and then resolve it with better ideas.

Coming to terms

To arrive at a consensus you need to really work hard and make sure all the people involved are on the same page. Consensus could mean different to a lot of people. For some they have come to consensus because the situation demanded and they had to agree and compromise. And for some they arrive at a consensus looking at the long term benefits the negotiation has to offer.

The best tool that is used to come to terms or consensus is by offering considerations. If you offer too many considerations, then you may not be left with anything. So you need to understand how much you could sacrifice and what you will get out of this in the long run.

Finalizing the terms

It is the change over from being broad to specific. Many deals get delayed or do not happen because, they do not know how to build an agreement or finalize the terms of the agreement. The terms of agreement should be done based on the consensus each party has arrived at in good faith. Enough attention should be made to minor details, as you may end up giving too much that has not been part of the deal at all.

Some times while negotiating you may feel that the job is done where in, but it was just a thought which came up in discussions. You cannot conclude based on certain assumptions or feelings unless it is mutually agreed upon based on certain open and loud statements made by either parties. At the same time you cannot feel that all the problems are ironed out since the terms of the agreement are finalized. Then you may be in a rude shock which may happen at a later stage. It is a good practice the terms are openly discussed and the information is shared across all the people involved at periodical interval.

Writing the terms

To make the deal successful you should make sure that all the terms of the agreement are written in proper format. It is fine to discuss about the terms at large, but it is final in all sense only when it is written and executed well. The written agreement should have details about the process how and when the deal will be executed.

You may even think of some popular formats to make sure the written terms of agreement are drafted professionally.

VOLUME 3

The Art of Negotiation – in any circumstances

CHAPTER 11

How to Succeed – in tough situations

Most of the times, everyone wishes to negotiate with trust in each other. However, in certain situations, they may resort to situations that are not fair practices. So you should be prepared for the worst situations and thinking that someone might workout negative ways while negotiating the terms. You could overcome this situation by preparing for the worst and understand what is really possible at all levels.

Comfort zone tactics

Imagine a situation where the other party is hesitant even to come out of their cabin to a common place to discuss further. In such cases, you could be as polite as possible and say that you will not comfortable dealing in such situation and request them to come to a common place. Every time being in a comfort zone doesn't happen, you should make some adjustments and proceed further thinking long term.

Some times in negotiations you will have mediators who deal the situations on behalf of both the parties. Believing in the mediator and being deaf to the situation will be a wrong thing to do. It may so happen that they may favor your opponent making you feel that they are working towards your benefit. In such situations, both the parties along with the mediator should think of some common terms where all the parties involved will benefit out of this arrangement. You should make sure that the mediator adheres to the terms as earlier agreed upon by all the parties concerned.

You may be forced by your opponent into a zone that may not be too comfortable to you. In such case, you will have an option either to acquaint with the conditions or express your inability to continue. You need not force yourself or make a false impression that you are comfortable. Instead, you could let the other party know that certain things cannot be accepted in a subtle way or by expressing strongly through certain actions.

Attacking in various ways

While negotiating you should make sure to look at the larger picture and not what the other person said about you. However it is not necessary that everyone involved may take this approach like you, so you need to be prepared well if such situation arises. You will come across many reasons why the other members engage themselves in personal verbal attacks, some of the reasons are mentioned below:

- They will think that by attacking on someone they will become superior and such situation will help them while negotiating.
- They will be worried about their self-esteem, so to play it safe they get into disputes just to make sure their weakness is covered.
- Within themselves they will feel that no one involved is giving them due respect.

So to avoid such situations, you should make sure that the first thing you do is to give respect to the other person from the start and make them feel that they are important. Sometimes they may even try to resist hard because you are trying to resolve an issue. To tackle such issues, you can divert their attention by making some subtle statements about what is important about the deal. At times personal attacks may work in your favor depending on the situation and who is on the other side.

If someone is frequently engaging in a personal attack, you will know what kind of people you are dealing with and the best ways to deal with them. If you maintain your stance and display maturity till the end, the other person who attacks you will feel bad over a period of time. Finally patience pays, you will be in a position of strength and without much discussion the deal may work in your favor.

Emotions and you

It is extremely important to have a hold on your emotions and it takes lot of maturity and overall understanding of the situation. In a negotiation it depends on how well you understand the other party on emotional lines and are you able to connect to them instantly. If the emotions are heating up during negotiations make sure you walk away from the situation for some time till it settles down.

Controlling emotions is not that easy. The more you try to get into it, you will only end up in damaging the result. Your only aim should be to make progress in any situation and benefit from it. And it will happen only if you control your emotions.

What is the best time to move out?

In real world not every negotiation ends in a positive result. If it happens every deal made till today would have been successful. Being realistic and aware of the situation you should weigh all options while looking at a deal. While you want the next best thing to happen, not all parties would be interested in fair practices or the way you wish to do business with them. A deal may not happen for various reasons and you will even get an indication when to walk off or call off the deal.

Some of the situations where the deal may be called off are:

- If your other party makes you really uncomfortable or threaten you with dire consequences.
- If your other party uses negative tactics on you to get control over the situations.

Do not feel that by walking away from the deal or negotiation makes you feel inferior to others. Instead, you should feel happy that you have done the right thing before further damage is done for everyone involved because of a few negative elements. So the decision you take today, will be of help to you tomorrow when situations are in your favor and everyone involved realizes what they did in the past.

Some parties use negative tactics and even may go the extent of threatening you because it would have worked for them in the past. Imagine if every time such situation arises, and every time you walk out then that situation may vanish. And if it is practiced by everyone, there could be an end to such kind of malpractice.

Winning and losing situations

The initial step in negotiations is that you should work out certain alternatives if the desired outcome fails to happen. If you are able to work out some alternatives, you will have lot of clarity while dealing in unknown and sudden outcomes. You will have lot of confidence and your view will be much realistic in nature. Let us look at some negotiation outcomes and how to deal with them.

Win – lose situation

A win lose situation offers a clear result. It is like the game of soccer finals, someone has to emerge as winners. The losers will definitely be disappointed and will not be able to come to terms with the winner now and also in the future.

Lose – lose situation

In this kind of situation the negotiation of one party happens as if there is no tomorrow and they try all ways and means to demean and defeat the other party. In trying to do so, they finally end up in losing because their aim will never to win but to make the other party lose. In this type of lose – lose situation none of them will win because their goals and objectives are either hidden or never met. And in extreme cases none of them meet again.

Win – Win situation

It is finding the right balance between what all the parties involved are looking for. It doesn't mean that if one party wins the other loses. The reason negotiations happen because there is a common objective that both the parties would like to achieve. Most of the successful negotiations end up in win – win situation as there are concessions, clear thoughts and a vision for long term perspective. It doesn't mean that a win-win situation happens to only one party and that they have one. It automatically means that both parties won and their objectives are met.

Null and void situation

This is a situation where no party wins or loses. Either party will find it difficult to deal with other as there is no consensus on even one point they discuss on. And they would never want to come back again. In such situations the parties look for someone else who would be interested in similar objective and will take it forward with them.

There is literally waste of time and resources as they spend lot of time on arriving at a consensus and then to find for alternatives in terms of people and places. The best way parties see in such situation is walking away from it. This may seem better as further damage is avoided for both the parties involved.

CHAPTER 12

What if you have to negotiate on somebody's behalf

The toughest job to handle is to negotiate on some ones behalf. You should know the exact price that the party is willing to offer the other party. And at the same time, keep it confidential till the last part of the negotiation. You should also know what kind of considerations are allowed by the party for negotiating further. There will some sensitive and tough questions that will be posed by other parties to you. In such cases, you should be aware of all the information and make sure that you don't cross the line of what your party expects from you.

The team composition

The negotiating team you choose makes the big difference in completing the deal. It all depends on how much information you would like to share with them. Transparency will play a key role in deciding the team's progress in negotiation. It is essential that you select the team based on their strengths and how they can complement their skills with each other. You should also make sure that the team meets periodically and do the following:

- Constantly remind the team of why they are together and remind them about the cause.
- Make sure everyone understands their job and works accordingly.
- Prepare a road map and plan to meet the desired objectives.

If your team has all of them thinking in different directions, you may still be able to take them forward. But it may take more time for them to settle down and understand the overall objective. But if you have a team that gels well and envisages the future they will be able to work towards the final outcome.

Each one has a responsibility

While negotiating it is important that everyone has defined roles. You cannot wear multiple hats and complete all the jobs on time. You need to have domain experts who handle specific situations and areas. However you can look at the overall composition and make sure the combination works.

You may even have a team who should be able to take certain decisions on their own. If they are given certain freedom they can do wonders and make sure that the deal is completed by all means. Your job will be to make sure that they do not over step and work out selfish ways to negotiate the deal. You need to balance every situation where the team is exposed and any mistake that happens you should be able to present an alternative strategy with immediate effect.

Once the responsibilities are given to the team, all the loose ends should be tied by you. Any shortfalls that the team may have should be guided by you and make them feel the overall objective of the negotiation.

How to answer something without answering

Any question that needs to be answered, should not be in a sense that it backfires you at some point of time. Below are some situations where you could use them to your benefit:

- If someone asks a question that is not part of the current situation, you could just put it back subtly to them saying that, "we should visit this area later, let us focus on the current aspect".

- If you are not aware of something and the other party asks you a question related to that, instead of making a wild guess and making it more embarrassing, you can simply tell them that you will get back to them in a day or two.
- If your answer reveals too much of information pertaining the current deal, then it is better to hide certain information and put it off for the time being.
- Once your answer is done, you may even pose one question to make sure that the other party is happy that you are interested in knowing more.

CHAPTER 13

Negotiations in International Business Scenarios

International business is related to the dealings that happen between countries at a personal level, country level and at government level. The corporate organizations or private institutions deal with such negotiations for their expansions and benefits. And governments deal with such business to improve their relationships between countries for certain political reasons. Some examples of international business are trade – import and export, direct foreign investments, franchise and licensing agreements.

Communication - different approaches

Communication plays a vital role in negotiations. It is with good communication that even a sensitive issue could be communicated with ease. As far as business is concerned communication happens between various people who are involved directly and indirectly. And effective communication will help the organizations representatives to fill the gaps that may arise while doing business.

In international business negotiations, communication happens at all levels cutting across different cultures and barriers. A company in the USA who is negotiating on certain terms with a company in Japan may have lots of communication barriers pertaining to culture and protocols. Organizations hire communication experts who are aware of all these barriers. These communication experts even know how to involve all the stake holders and make sure that the deal is closed.

If you are playing a role of a communicator involving international business negotiations you need to obtain the following traits:

- Be able to speak multiple languages
- Be able to understand country specific cultures and appreciate the same
- Be willing to travel and make sure the initial rapport is set up
- Understand the mindset of all the stakeholders involved
- Have a business understanding of the entire deal and be able to suggest
- Be able to take certain decision on the stakeholders behalf
- Display maturity in situations that deal with sensitivity

Negotiations and the negotiator

As far as negotiations at international level are concerned there are not fixed rules expect certain rules pertaining to the country's culture and trade policies. Negotiations on an international platform are based on the following:

- Be aware of the time zones and the right time
- Business environment and how it shapes up in the future
- People involved today and in the future
- Information – gathering and analysis
- Hierarchy – whom to approach the other side and how to deal with them

Globalization has affected the way business is done. And everyone wants to do business as of yesterday. And this has directly affected the way negotiations happen at international level. An important aspect of negotiation is to compromise on the location of the negotiation as it usually involves different countries and time zones. If you accept a particular location for negotiation then it is clear that there is some concession that you had opted for. For covering this up at a later stage you need to make sure that you earn some advantage for the concession made.

Negotiator

Negotiator could be anyone – a supplier, or a buyer, a seller or a customer, a superior or a subordinate, a businessman, a country's delegate or a diplomat. Negotiator plays different roles as far as international business is concerned. Most of the negotiators at this level have a strong positive attitude as they have seen business and relationships taking shape at all levels. They will see conflicts as a healthy approach and learn out of every situation they come across.

If you are playing the role of a negotiator at an international level, the first quality you need to possess is adaptability to any kind of situation. You need to be open to take up criticism and understand that you represent a larger fraternity and cause. You will be exposed to a lot of people and situations. You will not have time to experiment and then see how it works. Certain times, you will be altogether into a new situation that you have never experienced before. So it requires lot of patience and professionalism to handle a role like this. If you are allowed to choose a team working on negotiations your job will be a challenge to choose people of like mindedness.

There will be certain situations where no one can replace you and at the same time you would need more people to represent you in various locations. Ideal way of dealing with these situations is to select the team, groom them, set the expectations and do everything simultaneously.

Final few words

Every chapter you have read till now would have made you feel that you have mastered the art of negotiation under any circumstances. There are certain tips which you need to carry in your brain or at a handy place to make sure you follow these. The key portions of the book are here by summarized for your understanding. You may just recollect your memory cells and feel comfortable that you have known most of the points highlighted below.

Summarize – essential qualities of a Genius Negotiator

You are here to make the difference. A genius negotiator is the one who will make sure the desired outcome happens against all odds. The entire negotiation process could be crafted as a beautiful poem that sings along to find its destination. You will need to carry some of these behaviors to make sure that the tag of genius revolves around your head all the time.

- Showing compassion towards the other side and dealing the situation in your stride
- Being responsible for the entire process and making sure it works
- Showing due respect to the other party and understand what they have to say
- Being adaptable to any situation that you get into
- Dealing the entire process in all fairness
- Being honest and displaying highest level of integrity
- Patience is the name of the game and you understand it well
- Self-discipline: setting up the platform and leading by an example
- Being creative and witty
- High on energy till the last page is signed

Being a genius you wouldn't like to give up in between and you will make sure that the deal is closed in all possibilities there by ensuring highest level of trust is built.

Result oriented techniques – sum it up

Simple things that you follow could lead to extra ordinary results. While it is good to have a great plan in place, but what if the other person doesn't see the plan through your eyes. You need to make sure that plan comprehends to small pieces and sums up to the overall plan.

Try to create an atmosphere that is congenial and not too formal. For example, if you have too many physical blockades like chairs, tables or even temporary partitions in the area of your discussion, make sure you remove them. By doing so, you will make it easy for the other person who joins you in the negotiation and it will make them feel important as well.

Be informal in the initial stages and make them feel as if they are at their place. A few jokes may do the trick at times. Apart from this, you may also come across individuals who would like to visualize the future based on certain pictures which will capture their mind. So make sure that you show them some images that are in the current scenario and how they may change in the future once the negotiation happens.

Be sure to avoid these – a reminder

The major differentiator between happening and not happening could be the 'to avoid' aspects while negotiating. If you are negotiating on a deal and feel that you completed it successfully – suddenly you come to know that it has to be approved by someone else, how does it feel? You have wasted a lot of time by then. So make sure you reach the right person before it all starts – remember preparation. Be sure to avoid personal attacks and don't take them to heart. Avoid being rigid in the initial stages of negotiation, otherwise you will break the deal even before it happens.

Conclusion

Whatever negotiation situation you find yourself in, whether it's bartering for a piece of hand-made pottery in a foreign country, or putting your job on the line wanting to be promoted, you stand more chance of being able to influence the decision by thinking it out first. When you are ready, put your cards on the table and hope that they give the opposing party enough for them to consider your proposal. Where people go wrong is that they look at their own needs and forget that negotiation is a two way thing.

If bartering for something which has a high price, such as a house, it makes sense to start with a sensible though low offer and to use the negotiation table to come to a price which both parties agree on. However, never go above what you believe the house is worth. Some people negotiate and let emotions get in the way and that's when negotiations can go badly wrong. You want that house so much, you pay over the market value and still have repairs to do. That's not good negotiation. In fact, you lose out in the end because the market value is not going to change just because you put your heart where your head should be.

You can influence others when you learn about two sided negotiation because you are also learning about how human relationships work. In your negotiations, never forget that the final decision depends not just on you, but also on what is acceptable to the other party. Thus, be friendly. Always approach the negotiation table in a friendly and open manner because if you try to be hard or try to tell someone that what they are offering is not worth it, you may find that they take umbrage and will do no more negotiation with you because of your attitude.

People who learn to negotiate put themselves in a very powerful situation, where people do tend to listen to them, because they know that there is something in it for them. It takes humility, it takes understanding and it takes being able to listen to other people. Once you do, and you keep their point of view in mind as well as your own, you will find you are much more likely to win the day.

Free Bonus Video: Negotiating Strategies and Tactics

Here is a great video going over the fundamentals of negotiating - the critical skill; why everything is negotiable; determining what you really want; doing your homework; the keys to business negotiating; using power as a negotiating tool; how emotions can help or hurt you; developing options in negotiating; the element of time in negotiating; negotiating complex agreements.

Bonus Video: https://www.youtube.com/watch?v=O0eniBUBgD0

Check Out My Other Books

http://www.amazon.com/Master-Job-Interview-Proven-Techniques-ebook/dp/B00PFFK7EE/ref=sr_1_1?s=digital-text&ie=UTF8&qid=1422404201&sr=1-1&keywords=master+the+job+interview

www.ingramcontent.com/pod-product-compliance
Lightning Source LLC
Chambersburg PA
CBHW07084818180526
45168CB00002B/999